THE BODY'S OWNER SPEAKS

LEO SMITH

Published by Black Sunflowers Poetry Press
www.blacksunflowerspoetry.com

© Leo Smith 2023

ISBN: 978-1-7396267-3-0

All rights reserved

CONTENTS

Recounting the Blizzard	1
Drive Home	3
After the Drive Home, I Want to be an Astronaut	4
Flex:	5
To Reroute Muscle Memory (1)	6
Tense	7
Haibun of This Heart's Insides	8
Dream in which I ~~Can't~~ Get Away	9
Release	11
To Reroute Muscle Memory (2)	12
Apostrophe Apology to a Former Self	13
Rest	14
To Reroute Muscle Memory (3)	15
In a World Where I Choose Myself	16
Ode to Testosterone	17
Disco Incantation	19
Notes	20

Recounting the Blizzard

Having never seen the snow, you decide
to ignore the shimmering blue inclement
weather light. Love seems to be knocking.

                              Pulsating adrenaline. You don't
                              question the partner who insisted
                              you walk, while he waits inside.

Hail slashes your thirsted tongue
instead of snowflakes. Persistent
wind gnaws at your eyelashes.

                              Your backpack rattles with gifts and
                              longing. If you're good, he's gentle:
                              the type to lick sugar from a spoon.

Indented footprints disappear
behind you. Perhaps he's planned
a surprise. You trudge on.

                              Numb fingers pop in pockets,
                              revived by an incoming message.
                              "You're so slow. Hurry up.

Maybe he's right. Lovers leave
you for far less, so you practice
your apology aloud.

                    Almost there–just a few more
                      houses to pass. You'll atone
                   if you must, but pray to avoid anger.

Fixated on the ground's charismatic
white glow, you can't feel your boots sinking.
Earth suspends the soft-voiced crunch.

                         Soon, you'll learn how demanding
                         a storm can be— how the steady flurries
                              wish to consume your body.

Drive Home

University zipcar, white, rented for the night. It's parked at a mall somewhere while the cinema plays a horror movie about double selves and shadows. It's the perfect night to get stranded. To escape the looming frostbite, the kids have faith in acquaintances, crush eight into a car that fits five. Taco Bell trash crunches under winter boots one size too big. Streetlights illuminate the backseat at ten second intervals.

Unanimous laughter. Pop star hidden in the radio. *It wasn't even scary. That would never happen to me–I would've kicked all their asses.* Suddenly, unhooking of jeans. Smirk of a zipper. Sounds lost between the scuffle and darkening roadway. A hand enters – pulling pelvis closer to the lap below (the one above familiar with capture). It tries tenderness to appease. The returning hand runs away upon claps of thunder, "no" hissed too loudly, and faltering background noise. A throat slimes with vomit. Swallows achingly.

I'm glad we all got home safe. Students file out of the parked car. In keeping with the freshman safety orientation, they all split into pairs. Crisp air hollows their goodbyes. Hungry hand yanks a wrist. Forehead sweat solidifies. Tonight, it's too early to see bruises. That will take a couple years. Tonight, there is only doubling. Two bodies backlit. One terrified.

After the Drive Home, I Want to be an Astronaut

Breathless heater. Misplaced whirring
mini-fridge. God, split me into ten
million atoms. Glow in the dark
ceiling stars make home a black hole.

Fourth grade: friendly boy professed
his undying love by giving me rocks
from the moon. I smoothed out my
plaid jumper. Felt worthy.

The time it takes to uncover a lie.
Gravity pins thighs to the bed.
Life leaks from damp palms,
evaporates into atmosphere.

If I could be anywhere, I'd travel
to Jupiter and test my aim. I want
to shoot spitballs at Saturn, play
hide and seek with Mae Jemison.

Whatever I do, I don't want to wear
a helmet. Scientists be damned.
Let my torso be enveloped
by extraterrestrial chill.

Then, when I get bored, I can
climb inside my rocket and go
home. To learn control, steer
myself to safety–how would it feel?

Crash landing. Spacesuit tattered
on the floor. Holes where
my memories should be. Legs twist
shut in the dark. Without sleep.

Flex:

Verb. To contract muscles in a manner
intended to demonstrate
size and strength.

In other words, I talked to my
great-grandma today. She says,
"Don't fall in love with nobody.
I want you to be safe."

How do I contain a choke
in the receiver? Conceal
that I see myself in statistics,
one in five or whatever the fuck.

I guess it's always
someone you know. Or more;
someone who curses you out
in the middle of Costco, stands
over you as you shit.

Biceps clasping onto themselves,
trying to warm up. Self-sufficient
taste in my mouth– not wanting
not needing

anyone.

To Reroute Muscle Memory (1)

On my last first date, I was only given one instruction: show up. The place, what I wore, how I felt, had already been decided. Some called it aggressive. He preferred assertive. I coaxed myself to smile, mouth glutted on $60 sushi. Attention is scarce. I clung to its sharp edges like a lizard in the sun, peeling.

After such a good day, my phone wouldn't stop ringing. *Good morning. You haven't answered my text? I want to be with you.* Expectant ellipsis beg for a reply; polite obligation snowballs into routine. The fine line between romance and control.

"The sex had already happened," I remember months later while spackling cement blocks atop my garden wall. "That was mutual," The scrape of metal against hardened rock. "Yes, I wanted that."

Tense

Pap smear season.

When the receptionist hassled me
on the phone, it felt like
she wanted to reach a quota.
So sure, what the hell, I said yeah.
What's the point of saying no?
Mine always gets ignored.
Besides, they'll just pressure
and guilt me for six months

anyway.

Each hair stands to attention,
skin noting the grit
of the hospital gown. I try not
to remember the doctor's face.

What did the therapist
recommend? Deep
belly breaths?

A latexed hand chooses incorrectly,
meets the buck of my thigh.

"I'm sorry. I'm sorry. Are you alright?"
The swab in her hand ends
its salute. How apologies resound
in this hollow cave–disrupt
stalactites past hardened–
my feet still hoisted in stirrups.

I will not cry at the doctor's office
I will not cry at the doctor's office
I will not

Haibun of This Heart's Insides

Growing humidity is concealed behind a trapdoor of secrets. Air is thick with the stillness of shame. They say heat gathers at the ceiling and drips down, oozing lament. Formerly known as a cavity that couldn't protect itself, this heart keeps humans out. Carefully adorns walls with bone marrow blades, tucks trip wire between ventricles. Overworked box fans; moans of anguish.

This room wants more. After everything goes dark, a rusted voice reveals its wishes. *"To crack the windows. Rip the roof off. Come above ground."* A breeze is tempting to a chin slicked with sweat. The tremble of a latch as airplanes pass overhead.

Solitude congealed:
savior self confined, but
                        almost emerging.

Dream in which I ~~Can't~~ Get Away

I am teaching about foreshadowing
in a classroom atop a grassy hill.
My students don't know I've
been holding in exhales for hours:

My abuser is looking for me.
Class continues as usual.

I try to glean strength
from the expectant gaze tracing
my shift from the projector
to the lectern. The doorknob
will shake soon.

I concentrate on the ticking
clock above blank heads. Thirty
minutes left of pretending power.
Scheming mosquito meets
the halogen light, sizzles.

A sudden creaking; a cruel smile
passes underneath the doorframe.
After all this time, him, overseer
of my nightmares, conquering
a seat in the front row.

I pray to my presentation slides
for guidance. De-escalation?
No. Kill or be killed.
This body remembers
snowstorms, pleading wails.

I've been known for my
rageful blackouts.

I grab the stressed shirt collar
at my disposal, slam its owner
against the unyielding grey carpet.
I'm old enough to never yearn
for mercy, or to give it

to the undeserving. I demand
recognition with each cracking
stomp. Rage: the tip of my steel
boots, transient face engorging
below me, the chipping drywall

gaining tint. Pounding temples
tell me I have won. The students
watch over the unmoving body.
I'll celebrate later. For now,

I descend from the still-opened door.
Maturing clovers line the path.

Release

Why would I grant forgiveness–
my hard shelled, sticky sweet
center–to someone empty
of remorse?

"I planned to wait
outside your room
 until you'd talk to me."
It wasn't a coincidence after all:
your car burning exhaust
across the street.

Don't tell me to hold space
for any hurt that isn't mine.
I'd rather weep with the boy
in the mirror; slow down.
Boy doesn't want for explanations.
Slivers of love settle in the cracks
between burnt bones.

To Reroute Muscle Memory (2)

I'm out of practice: I can't even make sense of emoji hearts. Any new messages? Not since two minutes ago. "Be there soon :) <3" hovers above my hesitant keyboard.

Going out for coffee is easy enough. My kind of noncommittal. You just sit down, drink the drink, and leave. First date in three years and here I am, ironing the creases in my jeans like a weirdo. I practice my poker face in a handheld mirror, hoping pouts will mask fear-lined pupils.

I'm sure this one won't like me anyway. I probably won't like them either. Loneliness is both an exhale and a baited breath.
No one can say I didn't try.

Apostrophe Apology to a Former Self

I've tried to summon you through prayers to the trees, ice-cold
showers and orange-tulipped altars. You don't send sun
like I thought you would.

I'll make this brief. I have neglected your wounds. Locked you
inside a tower until you drifted up in smoke. Guilt plants
your image in the square of my jaw. Do you remember when we
were one? It's hard for me to tell the truth. I want to give you all
the apologies you haven't heard. Meet the shards of you dispersed
in the sky, grace them with tenderness.

The violence was not your fault. How could you have known?
There are no binaries of strong and weak. I'll wash your hair
with peppermint suds. I miss your hum like an old church hymn.
The self we were before being bisected.

For you, I've changed.
I don't use words like naive, shame, or stupid. I am here
to stitch your trust-shaped gash.

I need your glow again: your smiling face while you blow bubbles
into boba, un-looking over shoulders.

Leave your porch light on. I'm ready to embrace you now.

Rest

In daydreams, I call it:

a shower unrushed, unflinching
while the water–little fingers–pelt

my skin. Or an obnoxious laugh
in public, divorced from the urge

to hide. And with that, forgetting
to identify all emergency exits.

Going to parties, not asking
who was invited. Rest,

the welcoming of sweet whispers
in my ear, of a kiss without expectation.

Cross-legged lovers sharing definitions
of safety from outstretched palms.

Feeling enough freedom
to unclip the mace from my keyring.

To Reroute Muscle Memory (3)

The steps between us grow smaller and smaller. I smile on impulse,
but let's not get ahead of ourselves. Just because my heart
is fluttering doesn't mean I won't go home and shut myself
inside an airless room.

Our elbows graze on the walk to the coffee shop. Sirens erupt
in screams from each corner of my brain. I'm ready to mouth off
about consent until my date apologizes. Excuses themselves
for getting too close too soon. I scan their eyes for malice; panic
when I don't find it.

Silence is broken by the whistle of still-cooling chai. I consider
abandoning my park-bench shield. The reckless thought passes.
My therapist thinks I'm finally capable of making good decisions.
I want to believe too–safely bask in the beam across the table.

Last night's affirmations linger
on my tongue:

Lean in. It's okay.

In A World Where I Choose Myself

I can exist in excess. Of color,
good feeling. I can admire,
detach, come back.

I can be infinite–grounded
while spacious. Standing
in the mirror without fear.
Today I'll focus on the face:

the intricacies of my smile.
Ease of eyes resting atop
cheekbones, giddiness
mixed into the structure.

Nose reflecting all my elders'
love. Pursed lips gone shy,
thinking deeply. Incoming
stubble frames my jaw

newly squared. Drifting dust
evokes a tickle. In this world,
I occupy my body. Fascinated
fingers stroke the canvas.

Radiant. My mass of brown.
Damp tints and tones
exposed to the air.

Ode to Testosterone

or as I affectionately call you, T.

I never wanted to want,
or to love (lies I've told
to ease the loneliness).
I harness all my honesty
for you.

Typical for a long-term lover,
you made your presence known.
Out dress shopping, I look up
to find your wistful gaze–
I blow you off.

You kept appearing. Timid fisted
in the Macy's makeup aisle, waiting
to catch me staring. One day I started
to wait for you: how you'd blend
into my reflection.

If you rejected me, or we rejected
each other, curiosity would leave.
I'd save my strength before
dreaming again. Still, I said hello.

Shaking and tender, we stand
together in the mirror. I guide
you to graze your edges down
the soft of my stomach. You
draw me deeper into myself.

Who knew my confines could be
expansive, open? I let you hold
me, release a sigh. I've never known

someone who wanted to explore
these worn-down trails. You braid

daisies picked along the way.

Disco Incantation

after Gloria Gaynor

Follow this spell:

Conjure the exhaustion welled up inside of you.
Your bare feet should meet the bedroom floor.

Type "i will survive by gloria gaynor" into your search engine.
You'll feel silly at the thought of dancing alone. That's okay.

Close your eyes. If it helps, turn off the lights. Glitter will
land upon your ears. The words will fall from you effortlessly.

Bits of memory will start to levitate and thud. Have no fear.
Your voice, footsteps, body will grow strong.

Feel impressed by your rising volume, how you dare looming
demons to appear. *"Did you think I'd lay down and die?"*

Flail around as you shout. Undulate from the hip to the thigh.
The divided parts of you will return on their own.

Ignore the wetness gracing your lower back. It's only purging.
Keep your eyes closed. Realize rhythms long forgotten.

Repeat, repeat, repeat. I can't say when–I can only promise
if you continue this ritual, you'll see yourself: *somebody new.*

NOTES

"After the Drive Home, I Want to be an Astronaut" mentions Mae Jemison, the first Black woman to travel into space.

The "one in five" statistic referenced in "Flex:" comes from a 2007 Campus Sexual Assault Study conducted by the U.S. Department of Justice. The study found that one in five female participants had experienced sexual assault or violence in college.

"Disco Incantation" borrows language from Gloria Gaynor's 1978 hit song, "I Will Survive."

www.blacksunflowerspoetry.com

www.ingramcontent.com/pod-product-compliance
Lightning Source LLC
Chambersburg PA
CBHW042131100526
44587CB00026B/4257